6 DAYS TO BETTER GRADES

Powerful Study Advice
For All College Students

Dr. Jason A. Davies, Ph.D.

Published by CreateSpace Publishing

6 DAYS TO BETTER GRADES
- Powerful Study Advice For All College Students

Published by CreateSpace Publishing

ISBN 1438283369

To my parents
Gerald and Jennifer Davies

And in memory of
Daniel Benjamin Bartle,
24th May 1989 – 16th July 2008

5/11 B&T 9.17

Disclaimer

Every effort has been made to make this book an easy to follow guide to help you to achieve good grades at college. However, your level of success will depend upon: the time you devote to this book and the ideas and techniques described; your knowledge and various skills; the quality of your teaching, and many other factors. Since these factors differ according to individuals I cannot guarantee your success in achieving your goals. You use the information/ recommendations in this book at your own risk. Nothing works for everyone. What works for you may not work for someone else and vice versa.

The examples given in this book that contain a person's name are illustrative and fictitious. Any resemblance to real persons, living or dead, is purely coincidental.

Contents

Part One

Better grades in 6 days!

Day 1

Attitude and Confidence

Introduction

What do you think and feel when you hear the words: *Study* or *Revision*?

- You may see studying as a chore,
- You may think of it as something depressing,
- You may even find it frightening,
- You may think of studying as uncool,
- You may think that you can get by without studying,
- You may think that none of your friends study,
- You may see studying as something that should be avoided at all costs, until absolutely necessary, say, the week before your exams,
- You may try not to think about study at all.

All of these are *negative attitudes*.

Welcome to Day 1 of this course. Over the next 6 days I will show you that *study* and *revision* are nothing to be worried about and I will give you clear, simple, and practical study advice that will help you to achieve good grades at college.

Develop a positive attitude

Many students have an unhealthy attitude towards study and revision (in fact many students don't have a concrete idea of exactly what is meant by *study*), but think about this: your success, in anything that you attempt in life, is largely due to your attitude. A good attitude leads to good results, whereas a poor attitude leads to poor results. So why not develop a great attitude and get great results?

With the right attitude towards your studies, your confidence will grow, you'll find your work easier, you'll get your work done in less time, your marks will improve, and you'll enjoy your work more.

So how do you improve your attitude? Well, attitudes are nothing more than *habits of thought* and bad habits can be replaced with good ones.

Attitudes are... *habits of thought* **and bad habits can be replaced with good ones.**

If you have the habit of saying, "I hate studying," or "I'm bad at studying," or "I'm a poor student," then over time you will convince yourself that this is true and it becomes part of how you *define* yourself.

But remember, attitudes are simply *habits of thought*. So next time you find yourself thinking, "I hate studying," or "I'm bad at studying," or "I'm a poor student," then stop yourself and think instead, "I'm learning to like studying," and "I'm getting better at studying," and "I'm becoming a good student." Use this technique everyday.

Simply by developing a better attitude towards your studies you'll be amazed by how your confidence will grow and how the quality of your work will improve.

I'm going to set you a challenge: As you work through this book try to consider each lesson with a positive attitude. Try to take an *active* and *open-minded* interest, and say to yourself: "I can really benefit from this, I will do my best to learn all that I can from it."

Believe in yourself; learn to say "I can..."

As well as developing a positive attitude towards your studies learn to *believe in yourself*. When faced with a challenge don't say, "I can't...," ask yourself, "Why can't I...?" and, "How can I...?"

You should practice this technique not only with respect to your studies but also in other aspects of your life where you face challenges.

For example, instead of saying, "I can't do math," ask yourself, "Why can't I do math?" and, "How can I improve my math skills?"

Or instead of saying, "I can't write essays," ask yourself, "Why can't I write essays?" and "How can I improve my essay writing skills?"

Or, instead of saying, "I can't learn to drive," ask yourself, "Why can't I learn to drive?" and "How can I go about arranging lessons?"

Or, instead of saying, "I can't be the first person to walk on Mars," ask yourself, "Why can't I be the first person to walk on Mars?" and "How can I get to work for NASA?"

I am completely serious here; do you think Neil Armstrong had self-belief? Do you think he was a positive or negative thinker?

Do you see how this is a much healthier and more positive way of thinking?

What I'm saying is this: don't underestimate yourself or put yourself down, be positive and think "I can…!"

Do this regularly and it quickly becomes second nature.

Fact: *You are capable of far more than you know.*

Fact: *You are capable of far more than you know.*

Take responsibility for your learning

Often, students don't do as well as they can because they don't fully grasp that at college *their learning is their own responsibility*.

What do I mean by this? Well, think back to how you were taught at school:

At school your teacher asked the class questions, set exercises to be completed in class, and gave homework assignments to make you think about your work and to check that you understood it as you went along. It's likely that your teacher knew everybody's name and probably had a good idea of everybody's individual strengths and weaknesses. Also at school, your time was structured and organized for you into classes, sports periods, and perhaps also into private study sessions.

The way you learn at college however is somewhat different. Some of your time is still organized for you; you attend lectures, tutorials, seminars, and practical classes, and you participate in fieldwork etc. You are also assigned coursework.

The major difference at college is the role that your lecturers play in your learning; at college the task of a lecturer is to *help you to know what to study* and to *act as a pace setter* as you progress through your course. It is *your* responsibility to organize your study time, it is *your* responsibility to **At college, your learning is your own responsibility.** set yourself study objectives, and it is *your* responsibility to actively learn the material.

Think carefully about these differences, it is important to recognize them and to appreciate the *shift* in who is responsible for your learning. At college it is up to *you* to take control and to take the initiative.

I hope that this doesn't sound too heavy! My intention is not to scare you or stress you! Throughout this book we will discuss many study and revision techniques and I will explain to you exactly how to take responsibility for your learning. It's not difficult and it's nothing to be worried about!

Treat your study time as *An Oasis of Calm.*

During your time at college you will have many new experiences and grow in many different ways, and a lot of your time will be fairly chaotic and difficult to control. This can be a good thing; being able to *let go* and *go with the flow* can be very liberating and you can learn a lot about yourself and have great fun. In this chaos let studying be like an *oasis of calm:* something you have complete control over, something you can rely on, and even look forward to. Life is always about achieving balance.

Summary

At college, your success will depend largely upon your attitude, your interest, your enthusiasm, and your self-belief. Get these things right and you're 70% there. The extra 30% is *effective studying*. Throughout this book we will consider how to improve your study and revision skills. I will show you how to take responsibility for, and control over, your studies and how to be *active*, not *passive*, in your approach to your work.

Definition Sheet 1

Study

Before we go any further let me define exactly what I mean by *study*.

When you think about studying you probably get a mental image of sitting at your desk trying to understand and memorize your lecture notes. The reason why you might define study in this way is because for many students this is the only time and place where they feel that they actually *learn* about their subject.

However, I want you to think about study in a different way.

Let's define it as follows:
Study is *the application of the mind to the acquisition of knowledge.*

Therefore, you are studying whenever you are *actively trying to learn.*

You are studying whenever you are *actively trying to learn.*

From this definition if you take the right attitude and approach to lectures, tutorials, seminars, laboratory classes, field trips, writing up practical sessions, and completing set homework etc. then in all of these situations you are *studying*.

Many students do not take full advantage of these learning opportunities:

- Many students do not prepare for lectures, and when in lectures they will simply passively transcribe what is being said.
- Many students have a negative attitude towards tutorials and seminars and do not prepare well for them or take full advantage of these learning opportunities.
- Many students do not prepare well for practical classes and simply passively follow the instructions without thinking about how what they are seeing and experiencing relates to their studies. They usually try to finish and leave as early as possible.
- When tackling defined homework, many students do not take this opportunity to learn about and read around their subject. Nor do they consider carefully enough the feedback that they receive from the assessor for their marked work.

Recognize all of these situations as *golden opportunities to learn*.

You'll get a better idea of what I mean by *active learning* as we continue through this book.

Definition Sheet 2

Compulsory and Voluntary Study

Throughout this book I will occasionally make a distinction between *compulsory study* and *voluntary study*. Let's think about these terms:

Compulsory Study (*Stuff you have to do*):

This covers your time spent in classes (lectures, tutorials, seminars, practical classes, and field trips) and the time you spend dealing with defined homework or coursework.

Voluntary Study (*Stuff you choose to do*):

This covers the time you spend in private study; revisiting and organizing your lecture notes, reading recommended texts, preparing summaries of your notes, considering past examination papers, and preparing for your classes, etc.

Suggested Further Reading

On some of the days of this course I will suggest that you read one (or more) of the Further Reading lessons which can be found in Part Two of this book, but I am not going to suggest any further reading today.

In this lesson I have given you some of the most important information and advice that you will find in the whole of the course, so why not spend some time really thinking about what you've read today? In particular, I want you to think about the possibilities that life presents to you if you develop an *'I can...'* mentality and a *positive attitude* towards all of life's challenges and adventures!

Day 2

Get Organized!

Introduction

At times during your degree you may feel overwhelmed by the amount of work that you have to deal with. We all feel like this from time to time.

In this situation, the trick is not to panic or get stressed out, but to: *get organized!*

> **Question:** How do you eat an Elephant?
> **Answer:** One bite at a time!

When trying to deal with a large task or assignment it is much easier to deal with a clearly defined sub task than to try to deal with the task as a

When trying to deal with a large task or assignment it is much easier to deal with a clearly defined sub task than to try to deal with the task as a whole.

whole.

The key piece of advice that I am going to give to you today is: when you are faced with a large task, break the task down into smaller, clearly defined, *subtasks* (tasks that you will be able to complete in about thirty minutes to an hour) and deal with each of them one at a time.

The ability to break large tasks down into smaller ones, which can be tackled in about thirty minutes to an hour, is an extremely useful skill - it is one of the cornerstones of this course.

Organize your study sessions using your notebook

Yesterday I promised that all of the study advice that I give to you in this book would be practical. So how do you put this particular piece of advice into practice?

Well, all you need is a *notebook* and a *pen*.

If you use your notebook effectively then it will become invaluable in organizing your studies.

My notebook

As I write this lesson I am sat at my desk typing on the computer with my own notebook open next to me. In my notebook, I write down all of the tasks that I need to complete and any relevant ideas that I have as they occur to me. The tasks that I need to deal with (and which tasks have priority) can change on a daily basis, but everything that needs my attention is there written down.

On a shelf in my office I have a whole series of such notebooks stretching back to when I was an undergraduate just like you. My notebook is an indispensable tool for organizing the tasks that need my attention on a day-to-day basis.

Break large assignments down into smaller, easier, sub-tasks.

Take your notebook to all of your classes, and when you are given an assignment turn to a clean page and write down the details of the assignment at the top.

Then, as soon as you can after class (the same day is best), spend half an hour breaking this large task down into smaller ones and list each of these sub-tasks on the same page in your notebook.

Let me give you an example:

Imagine you are given one week to write and submit an essay. There are a number of ways you could approach this assignment. Before we consider a good way of tackling such an assignment let's think about the way in which a poor student may approach it. We'll call this student Chris.

Chris's approach (a poor approach to tackling an essay assignment).

> The day the assignment is set Chris thinks, "A week is a long time! I'll get around to writing that essay soon."
>
> After a few days the assignment begins to weigh on Chris's mind a little and he begins to feel a bit stressed

about it. He dismisses these feelings and thinks to himself, "I've still got time. I'll get around to it soon."

As the week progresses the assignment starts to weigh more and more heavily on his mind and this makes him feel miserable. While Chris is doing the things which he usually enjoys such as spending time with his friends, watching television, playing sports, playing video games, or surfing the net, etc. - he finds it hard to enjoy himself.

As time goes on, Chris feels stressed and guilty, and he tries to push the assignment to the back of his mind.

Finally, it's the day before the assignment must be submitted, so Chris braces himself and reluctantly trudges to his room, sits down, takes a deep breath, and faces it. Because Chris hasn't thought about the assignment at all since it was set, it takes him some time to get into the swing of it. He is stressed, frustrated, and feels stupid because he can't figure it out immediately. Chris then spends four muddled and depressing hours, late into the night, getting it done. When he finally finishes the assignment he knows that it is far from what he is capable of.

What a *miserable* approach.

In contrast to this, let's now consider a much healthier and more positive approach to tackling such an assignment.

A good approach to tackling an essay assignment

On the day that the essay is set spend half an hour breaking this large task down into smaller tasks. Your list of sub tasks could look something like this:

a. Think about the essay

In this session you should spend some time considering what is required and make some notes on what you think should be included in your essay.

b. Do some background reading

You should use this study session to go to the library and carefully select and read some relevant passages from textbooks that will help you with your essay. Also, spend some time looking up relevant internet sources for information and ideas.

c. Prepare a plan

In this study session list all of the main points that you wish to make in your essay. Then make some additional notes on how you plan to expand on each of these points. Each of the points you make will form a paragraph in your essay.

d. Write the essay

In this session write your essay working closely to your plan.

e. Check the work

Finally, you should spend a study session ensuring that your essay answers the question that was set and that it is the best you can do.

These tasks should be spread out over the whole of the week. Considered individually each task is straightforward and should be easily within your ability.

Using your notebook

Your notebook is where you will clearly list all of the tasks that need your attention.

Don't get into the habit of writing things in rough on loose bits of paper and then copying them neatly into your notebook as this is a waste of time, and you're likely to end up with reams of paper scattered around your work space that you haven't got around to writing into your notebook!

Your notebook is where you will clearly list all of the tasks that need your attention.

Your notebook will never be assessed, you never have to hand it in; it's yours. No one need ever see your notebook. It can be as neat as you like or as messy as you like. Allow yourself to make mistakes and cross things out and have arrows here and there where you've written things in the wrong place. The important thing is not neatness but that your notebook makes sense to you.

Adding a task to your notebook means you won't forget it. It means that you have taken control of it and you have it in hand. You are then free to concentrate on other things that need your attention.

When you have completed a task tick it off or put line through it. Crossing off each task as it is completed will give you a sense of satisfaction.

Only schedule your study tasks one day in advance

Another suggestion I would like to make with regard to

organizing your studies is that you *only schedule your study tasks one day in advance.*

In your notebook you may be tempted to write down the date and time that you are going to tackle each of your tasks, but I suggest that you only plan one day in advance. At the end of every evening take out your notebook, read all of the tasks that need your attention, and choose which tasks you will complete the following day.

There are a number of reasons I suggest this:

- Planning just one day ahead means that you are less likely to have something unexpected turn up which interrupts your plans.
- By planning just one day in advance you will have a good idea whether you will feel like tackling something difficult the next day or whether you would like to take it easy and do a task that you enjoy.
- If you plan too far in advance then higher priority tasks may come up resulting in a lot of messy rescheduling.
- Planning one day in advance means that you can concentrate on the most important, or most urgent, tasks first.
- Planning one day in advance means that you begin thinking about a task the evening before you tackle it. This means that you get to 'sleep on it' and the next day you will have to struggle less to motivate yourself.

In the front of your notebook it's a good idea to keep a copy of your weekly timetable showing all of your classes. Then each evening, when you're scheduling tasks for the following day, refer to your timetable and decide when in the day you plan to tackle them.

Find and use *hidden hours* in your timetable to study

Let me talk to you a little more about finding time to study.

One of the difficulties in finding time to work is that your evenings are precious to you and you may wish to spend that time with your friends, doing things that you enjoy. It is hard to give this time up.

The good news is, however, that there are times of the day where there are opportunities to work which you may not have considered:

- Consider going to the library early in the morning for an hour or so before your classes start. The morning is the time that most people find it easiest to work effectively.
- Use the time during the day between your classes. You'll be surprised by how much you can get done in as little as 30-40 minutes (this is about the length of time you would be given to complete an essay question in an examination, for example).
- Consider going to the library immediately after your classes each day for an hour or so.
- Cut down on the amount of television that you watch. Use this time to get some work done and then go and do something more sociable.
- Consider getting up an hour or so earlier on Saturdays and Sundays to get some work done.

Treat the things you enjoy doing as *rewards* for working hard

Finally, treat the things that you enjoy doing (such as playing sports, going out with friends, telephoning home, and watching television etc.) as *rewards* for completing your study tasks. I guarantee that you'll enjoy the time that you spend with your friends much more if you know that you've earned it.

You'll enjoy the time that you spend with your friends much more if you know that you've earned it.

Whilst completing a study task think about the reward that you will give yourself afterwards; this will help you to stay motivated and enthusiastic throughout the task.

Summary

By way of a summary, let's consider a week in the life of a student (we'll call him Pete) who understands and practices the simple techniques we've discussed today.

Pete's week

Monday and Tuesday

Pete schedules his study time a day in advance. He completes all of the study tasks that he set himself on Monday and Tuesday and is pleased with the work that he gets done.

Wednesday

On Wednesday evening Pete gets a text message from his friend inviting him to the cinema on Thursday evening. Pete quickly looks at his college timetable in the front of his notebook and decides to get up an hour earlier on the Thursday morning to go to the college library. He also decides to use one of the free periods in the morning to work and also to stay an hour after his classes have finished to complete some study tasks; this frees up his evening. Pete replies to his friend saying, "Yes I'd love to come, I'll be a little late though, I won't be able to meet you at 6 but I'll be there at 7 in time for the film." His friend says, *that's fine* and is really pleased that Pete can make it.

Thursday

Pete completes his morning and evening study sessions in the library. He is looking forward to going out with his friends and is motivated to get his work done by thinking of the trip to the cinema as a reward.
He has a great time with his friends that evening and just before going to bed he spends ten minutes looking through his notebook and chooses which tasks he will tackle on Friday and decides when in the day he will do them.

Friday

Pete works hard at college and he makes good use of his free periods during the day to study. Also, he has scheduled two study sessions for the evening. This is fine because there's nothing good on TV anyway. At the end of the evening he takes out his notebook and schedules his work for the next day. He has planned to go out with his friends on Saturday evening so he schedules all his study sessions for the morning and early afternoon.

Saturday

Pete gets up at 8am and completes two half-hour study sessions before going for a run. He does another two sessions before lunch and two more sessions after lunch. By three o'clock he's finished studying for the day and is looking forward to going out in the evening with his friends. Just after he finishes his last piece of work Pete clears his study area and schedules study tasks for the following day. He doesn't expect to be at his best on Sunday morning, so he only schedules study sessions for the afternoon.

Pete is really pleased with all the quality studying he's achieved this week and meeting his friends feels like a good reward.

Sunday

Pete has a lie in on Sunday morning and then goes out for lunch, after which he completes the study sessions that he planned and gets an early night.

Monday

On Monday morning Pete is given an unexpected assignment that must be completed by Friday. He has other tasks in his notebook that need his attention, but this new assignment has priority. Pete is confident that by breaking this large task down into smaller ones, scheduling them one day in advance, and by making good use of the time available to him between classes, then he will be able to do his best work and that the assignment will be submitted on time. His confidence in his abilities as a student continues to grow.

In the above example, on Wednesday evening Pete had a text message from his friend asking him if he wanted to go to the cinema on Thursday. Consider this: What if Pete's friend had asked him to go out *that night* (the Wednesday) but Pete had study sessions scheduled? What should he do? Should he go out with his friends or stay in and complete the planned sessions? *What would you do?*

Well firstly, let me say that at college you will have to make sacrifices in your social life if you are to achieve a result that reflects your ability. *However*, your social life *is* important. If it is possible to reschedule the study tasks that you have planned in order to go out with your friends then this can be the *right decision*. Do not feel guilty about this; if you constantly say to your friends that you can't come out because you're staying in to study then one day they'll stop calling.

Your social life *is* important... if you constantly say to your friends that you can't come out because you're staying in to study then one day they'll stop calling.

It's often very unpleasant to be in studying when your friends are out. This can make you feel really miserable which can cause the quality of your work (and your attitude towards your work) to suffer.

You can help to avoid this unpleasant situation arising by:

- Dealing with your assignments well before the deadline. By doing this you should not be in a position where you are tackling an assignment that needs to be submitted the following day - such a study task cannot be re-scheduled.
- Making good use of your less sociable hours to study, such as in the morning before your classes begin and between your classes during the day. This will free up time in the evening.
- Specifying to your friends a number of evenings each week when you will be studying so that they know not to disturb you.
- Scheduling lower priority study tasks (ones that can be re-scheduled without too much trouble) for the evenings when your friends are *likely* to call.

This *positive* and *active* approach means that you *take control* of your studies.

Following the simple methods that I have described to you today will reduce your stress levels and improve your confidence as a student. Also, you won't have to worry that an assignment won't be in on time or that your work won't do you justice.

So, if you don't have a suitable notebook for organizing your studies then go out and buy yourself one today. Then paste or draw a copy of your college timetable into the front. If used correctly you'll find this is an indispensable tool for organizing your study tasks.

Suggested Further Reading

To complement today's lesson, you may wish to read:

Further Reading I: The study session

Day 3

Getting the most out of your classes

Introduction

Today we will talk about how best to approach your classes:

- Your lectures,
- Your tutorials and seminars,
- And the practical aspects of your course.

We will discuss *preparing* for your classes, how to take an active approach *during* your classes, and I will make suggestions for things that you can do *after* class to help fix your work in your mind.

For the duration of today's lesson don't worry about when you will fit these extra study activities in; we will go into detail about this on days four and five.

Lectures

Lectures are the principal way in which you are taught, so it's vital to have a good attitude and approach to them.

Before we consider a good approach to lectures, let's imagine the way a poor student might approach them. Let's call this student Joanne.

Lectures are the principal way in which you are taught.

Joanne's approach

Joanne starts the semester with good intentions of attending every lecture but ultimately she'll miss about 20% of them. She copies up some of the lectures that she misses straight away, but there are still several gaps in her notes. Her plan is to photocopy someone else's lecture notes when the exams get close.

Joanne keeps her notes in a drawer in her room and she tells herself that one day she'll get round to sorting them into their respective courses. She never prepares for upcoming lectures and rarely revisits her lecture notes or adds to them after class. Maybe, as examinations approach, in a last ditch attempt to understand the course she might, just might, read one of the recommended texts.

Because of this attitude Joanne never really understands what is said in her lectures and simply passively transcribes what the lecturer is saying. She tells herself that when it gets close to the exams she'll then get all her notes together and read through them in order to try to figure out what the lecture course is all about.

This passive, careless approach to lectures means that Joanne squanders these extremely valuable opportunities to learn. It means that she will have to put in a great deal of effort and suffer a lot of stress and anxiety when her examinations approach in order to attempt to assimilate all of the information. It also means that she cannot possibly do herself justice.

I'm sure that many of you will recognize some aspects of your own approach to lectures in this example. I know that I made many of the same mistakes as 'Joanne' in my first year at college.

However, by following the simple steps I will explain below, regarding your attitude and approach to lectures (*before*, *during* and *after* each lecture), you can dramatically reduce your last minute effort and stress and achieve a grade that better reflects your ability.

Before

To make note taking easier in class look at your syllabus beforehand, think about the topics that are coming up, and do some preliminary reading. Make sure that you understand all of the preceding lectures and try to appreciate how the upcoming lecture fits into the course.

During

During the lecture listen *actively* not *passively*. Having done some preliminary reading you can concentrate on listening to and understanding what is being said. You can take a critical interest and carefully select and record the main points that the lecturer is making. Try to relate what is being said to what you already know. Try to anticipate what the lecturer will talk about and try to appreciate his/her approach.

After

To make sure that you understand the lecture and how it fits into the course, revisit your lecture notes after class. The *revisiting* technique is another cornerstone of this course; we will go into detail about this on Day 4.

During the lecture listen *actively* not *passively*... [then] revisit your lecture notes after class.

Missing a lecture

Missing a lecture can have a knock on effect on subsequent lectures. Because your understanding is lessened, the quality of the notes you make in subsequent lectures will be affected.

If you skip a lecture and copy someone else's notes, you may miss something that the lecturer drew particular attention to that may not be sufficiently conveyed in the notes that you copy.

If, for some reason, you miss a lecture unavoidably then try to get the notes copied up as soon as possible. If there is anything you do not understand then ask another student or consult a textbook. If you still do not understand then speak to your lecturer.

Summary

- Prepare for and attend all of your lectures,
- Listen actively and make good notes,
- Then revisit your notes soon after class.

By approaching your lectures in this way you will have an excellent foundation for dealing with your tutorials, seminars, and practical classes.

Tutorials and Seminars

Often the topic to be discussed in your tutorial or seminar will be prearranged. You may have been issued with a syllabus, or a tutorial/seminar booklet for example detailing what will be covered in each session. Using these resources, do some preparation beforehand so that you will be ready to take part in any discussions.

Tutorials and seminars are a good opportunity to clear up any difficulties you may be having or to seek advice. Try to take an active part in the discussion. Ask questions and listen carefully to what everyone has to say; you may be surprised by how much you can learn from the contributions of other students.

Many students find tutorials and seminars quite stressful and unenjoyable – however, they are a compulsory part of the course so work on developing a *positive attitude* towards them. If you can do this then they will become less stressful and you should find them a valuable aid to your learning.

[Tutorials and seminars]... are *rich learning environments*... think of them as *short cuts to learning*.

In tutorials and seminars your mind is stimulated in many ways: you learn by talking, reading, writing, observing, listening, and thinking; they are *rich learning environments*.

Because of this you can learn a lot in a relatively short period of time so take full advantage of them. Think of them as *shortcuts to learning*.

Also, don't be afraid to ask what you think are silly questions. If you are thinking something then it is likely that there are others thinking it too!

Any notes that you make in your tutorials and seminars should be added to your lecture notes so that all your notes on each topic are in one place.

Practical classes/ Fieldwork

Preparation is the key to making the most of a practical class or a field trip. Read the practical script beforehand and make the connection in your mind between the experiment and what you have learned in your lectures and in your studies. Do not treat them as separate. Seeing things for yourself is a great way to learn providing you *understand* what you are seeing. Good preparation helps you to do this.

> **Preparation is the key to making the most of a practical class or a field trip... make the connection in your mind between the experiment and what you have learned from your lectures and in your studies.**

Many students do not read the practical script beforehand and then in the session they will passively follow the instructions as quickly as possible in order to leave early. They will often not understand what they are doing or why they are doing it. They will only consider what the practical was about when they get around to writing it up. Develop a better attitude.

Ask yourself, "What is the point of practical sessions?" Well, practical sessions are to help you to *develop your hands-on skills* and to *confirm for yourself* the things that you have been told in your lectures. Many college courses have no practical content as such. If yours does then you are very fortunate to have this extra method of learning - take full advantage of it.

Having thought about the purpose of the practical session or field trip beforehand, you can think carefully during the session about what you are doing and consider how it relates to what you have learned.

Writing up

Ideally, the neat notes you prepare whilst carrying out the experiment (date, title, materials, methods, and observations) should be the ones you submit in your write-up. If you re-write your practical notes then you may make mistakes during copying. It is not always feasible to submit your original notes, but it is good advice and will save you time.

In practical classes you may finish your investigation before the time is up. Use this valuable time to ask questions and to begin work on your write-up.

Remember, as with any large task, the best way to deal with writing-up a practical session is to break the task down into smaller, easier, sub-tasks (each of which will take you between thirty minutes and an hour to complete). In this instance your list of sub-tasks may look something like this:

1. Think about the write-up

> Think about the experiment and consider what is
> required in your report. Prepare some preliminary
> notes of ideas and information that should be
> included.

2. Do some background reading

> Go to the library and look up any references cited in
> the practical script. Also, look at relevant textbooks
> and internet sources in order to get more information
> and ideas.

3. Prepare a plan

> List all of the main points that you wish to make in
> your *discussion* and *conclusion* sections along with
> additional notes on how you plan to expand on these
> points.

4. Write the write-up

> A practical write-up usually contains the following:
> date, title, abstract, introduction, materials, methods,
> observations, discussion, conclusions, and references
> (some of these sections may be omitted. The person
> marking your practical script will be able to advise you
> on this).
> It is important that your write-up stays within the set
> word/page limit. If you do not know what this is then
> ask.

5. Check the work

> In this session you should check your write-up
> ensuring that it is the best that you can do.

Suggested Further Reading

To complement today's lesson you may wish to read the following two lessons:

Further Reading II: Dealing with coursework
Further Reading III: Writing Essays

Day 4

Term-time study: Weekdays

Introduction

Think about a typical week during term time. Once you take away the time spent in classes and dealing with defined homework, then the time you have left is your *free time*.

It is *you* who chooses how to use this time. It is *you* who chooses how much of this time to devote to voluntary study. It is *how* you choose to use this free time and how *effectively* you use it that will ultimately determine your level of success.

It is *how* you choose to use [your] free time and how *effectively* you use it that will ultimately determine your level of success.

Welcome to Day 4. Over the next two days I'm going to describe to you *six* voluntary study activities. If you do them regularly they will dramatically improve your understanding and will help you to be well prepared for your exams.

Today we will discuss *three* voluntary study activities that I suggest you complete on *weekdays* during term time. Tomorrow we will discuss three voluntary study activities that I suggest you complete on *weekends* during term-time.

On weekdays during term time find time to:

1. Revisit the day's lectures,
2. Read recommended texts, and,
3. Prepare for your classes.

(All of the tasks that I suggest today are designed to be achievable within 30 minutes to an hour. Therefore these tasks can be scheduled using your notebook exactly as we've discussed previously.)

I'll describe each of these activities in turn.

1. Revisit the day's lectures

Many students copy their lecture notes out neatly in the evenings, and they firmly believe that this helps them to learn their work. Many other students, however, are equally passionate that it is a waste of time.

Personally, I believe that if you prepared for the lecture and were thinking and selecting carefully during the lecture then your notes should be neat and well-organized. Therefore simply copying your notes out again is not of great benefit. It is a *passive* activity that doesn't stimulate your mind, in fact your mind could well be on other things.

Consider the *revisiting technique* that I describe here:

The Revisiting Technique

Revisit each of your lectures after class, preferably on the same day. I suggest that you spend about thirty minutes revisiting each of your lectures.

Clarify

Make sure that your notes are clear and correct, and draw attention to the most important points by highlighting, boxing, or underlining them.

Re-represent

An excellent aid to learning is to try *re-representing* the information in your lecture in a more *creative* way. In each revisiting session try representing your lecture as a *spider diagram*, or as a *table*, or as a *flow chart*, or as an *annotated diagram*, or as a bullet pointed *list* with headings and sub-headings etc.

An excellent aid to learning is to try *re-representing* the information in your lecture in a more *creative* way.

My personal favorite out of these options is the spider diagram. In order to create a spider diagram take a clean sheet of paper and write the title of the lecture (or the main topic covered in the lecture) in the center of the sheet inside a circle. Then add radiating lines from this circle linking the title of the lecture to the topics that were covered in the lecture. You can then add further lines radiating from these headings which link to sub-headings. Once you have done this add your own thoughts and observations, for example you may see connections between the headings/sub headings on one leg of the spider diagram and headings/sub headings on another leg, if so, then join them together with a line and write on the line why you think they are connected.

You can add as much or as little detail to this diagram as you like, but bear in mind that you are not trying to re-write everything that was covered in the lecture! The idea is that each of the points in your diagram acts as a *memory prompter;* reminding you of a chunk of your notes. The completed diagram helps you to see the topic as a whole. It also helps you to distinguish the main (more important) points covered in the lecture from the supporting details.

Many students find creating spider diagrams useful, whereas other students do not. If they don't suit the way you think about your subject - then try something else.

Representing your notes in one or more of the ways listed earlier helps you to recognize the *patterns, connections*, and *associations* within your work, which in turn helps you to *learn* and *remember*. This is *active* study; you are thinking, selecting, recognizing patterns, drawing, and writing.

Remember, examination questions usually require you to demonstrate your understanding by showing that you have recognized patterns and connections within your work. Rarely do examination questions simply require you to regurgitate chunks of information exactly in the same order that it was given to you in the lecture.

Recall

At the end of your revisiting session, put your notes to one side and try to recall the main points from memory.

Any notes that you make in your revisiting session should be stored with your lecture notes on the same topic so that all your notes are in one place.

2. Read recommended texts

As well as spending time revisiting your lecture notes, set aside a few weekday study sessions to look up the references mentioned in your classes.

Once you have selected a book, read *actively* not *passively*. For example, when you're trying to learn from a passage in a textbook don't simply read and re-read the passage over and over again in the hope that the information will stick. After the second reading or so you will struggle to maintain focus and your mind may wander to other things. Simply reading and re-reading a passage is a relatively ineffective - inactive - way of learning.

Active reading

Make your reading *active*. As with any study session: *specifically define your objective*. For example you may be looking for a specific fact or piece of information, or you may be trying to get a better understanding of an aspect of your work. Keep this objective in the front of your mind as you read; it's very easy to allow yourself to leisurely flick through a book looking at the pictures and reading the passages that catch your eye, but this would largely be a waste of time. Define your objective and stick to it.

Once you have chosen a book that fits your purpose, take a clean sheet of notepaper and clearly define your objective at the top. Then, note the title, the author, and the edition of the book that you have chosen and list any relevant page numbers so that you can find the same paragraphs if you need to refer to them again at a later date.

Consider this sequence when reading:

1. Read the selected passages quickly once. On this first reading pay particular attention to any headings and subheadings in order to get a feel for how the information is organized. Also, carefully read the first line of selected paragraphs as this usually tells you what the paragraph is about. After this first reading stop and think about what you have read.

   Read the selected passages quickly once... then, re-read the passages again slowly and critically... on the third reading, make notes.

2. Re-read the passages again slowly and critically. Then stop and think again about what you've read and re-read your objective.

3. On the third reading, make notes:

   - Try representing the information in a different form such as a flow chart, or a spider diagram, or as a list etc.
   - Try making concise, direct summaries in your own words.
   - Finally, highlight the important points in the notes that you have created and add your own comments and thoughts.

The notes that you make in this session should be filed with your lecture notes on the same topic.

Read beyond the recommended texts

I hope that I have conveyed to you by now the importance of having a positive attitude towards your studies. The students who do very well in their degree usually have a *genuine interest* in and a *real enthusiasm* for the subject that they are studying. In addition to reading recommended texts, you can help to stimulate your own interest and enthusiasm for your subject by reading magazines and journals that are relevant to your course. Also, there are likely to be books available about your subject of study that have been written for the general public; these books are usually written in an engaging and stimulating way, and they may help you to see your course in a fresh light.

3. Prepare for your classes

The third and final task that I will suggest to you today is to *prepare for your classes.*

Prepare for your classes... this preparation shouldn't take you long, and it will help you to keep a keen and active mind in your classes.

Allocate a few study sessions each week during term time to preparing for your lectures, your practical classes, your seminars, and your tutorials. You may be *required* to do some preparation for some of your classes; for example, you may be required to prepare an essay or a presentation for an upcoming tutorial. Even if you are not given a specific task to complete in preparation for a class, it's a good idea to spend some time thinking about and preparing for *all* of your upcoming classes.

You will probably have been given: a syllabus for each of

your lecture courses; a practical booklet detailing the experiments that you will be conducting in your practical sessions; and booklets detailing the topics to be discussed in your seminars and your tutorials. Use these resources to help in these study sessions.

In these sessions you should think about the topics that are coming up, consider how they relate to what you have previously learned, and do some preliminary reading.

This preparation shouldn't take you long, and it will help you to keep a keen and active mind in your classes.

Summary

So, to summarize this lesson:
On weekdays during term time find time to:

- Revisit your lecture notes,
- Read recommended texts, and,
- Prepare for your classes.

On Day 5 of this course I will describe to you three study activities to complete each weekend during term time.

Suggested Further Reading

There is no suggested further reading to complement today's lesson.

Day 5

Term-time study: Weekends

Introduction

In yesterday's lesson I described to you three study activities that I suggest you complete on *weekdays* during term time. Today I will describe to you three study activities to complete each *weekend* during term time. Again, if you do these tasks regularly they will improve your understanding and will help you to be well prepared for your examinations.

On weekends during term time find time to:

1. Organize your notes,
2. Create study cards, and
3. Familiarize yourself with past examination papers.

1. Organize your notes

The first study activity that I recommend you do each weekend during term time is to organize your notes.

Each weekend, spend half an hour or so ensuring that your notes are *up to date*, *well organized*, and *filed sensibly*.

Each weekend, spend half an hour or so ensuring that your notes are *up to date, well organized* and *filed sensibly*.

Providing your notes are arranged so that you can find specific notes as and when you need them, and you can add extra information when necessary, then that's fine (a cheap and simple system that allows you to do both of these things is to store your notes using ring binders/lever arch files).

At the front of your notes for each of your courses keep a copy of the course syllabus/course outline. At the back of your notes for each course keep copies of the relevant examination papers from the last two or three years.

Your notes are truly irreplaceable and you must therefore store them in a safe place. If a friend misses a lecture or two and asks to borrow your notes then go with them to make a photocopy or sit with them and get on with some other task while they copy out your notes. You cannot afford to lose them.

2. Create study cards

Also on weekends find time to *create study cards*.

Weekends are an excellent time for you to review each of your courses as a whole. To help you do this look back at your lecture notes, and at any additions that you have made, and use them to prepare study cards.

Weekends are an excellent time for you to review each of your courses as a whole.

You can buy packs of record cards (125 x 75mm) cheaply at most stationers. They are very useful for preparing concentrated revision notes such as:

- Lists of basic ideas,
- Concise summaries,
- Chemical reactions,
- Mathematical derivations,
- Quotes,
- Topic outlines,
- Annotated diagrams,
- Definitions,
- etc.

Each list, summary, outline, diagram, definition, etc. should be written on an individual index card. Because of their size, it's possible to carry a few cards around with you in your pocket or purse/handbag so that you can read them whenever you have a few moments to spare. These cards will prove particularly valuable in the weeks leading up to your exams.

Only write the *essentials* of each topic onto your study cards. By doing this, each card will act as a *memory prompter;* reminding you of a chunk of your notes. Creating study cards helps you to organize your knowledge, and helps you to see how each of the aspects of your work fit together to form the whole.

Preparing revision aids makes you think about each aspect of your work and helps you to recognize connections and patterns. Preparing study cards is far more mentally stimulating than simply reading through your notes – it is *active study*.

3. Familiarize yourself with past papers

Finally, find time each weekend during term time to familiarize yourself with past examination papers.

As early on in a lecture course as possible make copies of the relevant examination papers for at least the last two years. Copies of these can usually be found in your department's library or on your department's website.

Take care though; don't go back too many years because you may waste time looking at papers which were set when the syllabus was different or which were set by a different examiner. If your lecturer (who is usually the person who writes the examination paper) has changed in the last couple of years or if the syllabus has recently changed then this may mean that there are no (or very few) relevant past papers for a particular course. In this case your lecturer should be able to provide you with at least one specimen paper or a list of specimen questions for you to practice.

Each weekend during term time spend some time considering the past paper questions. Obviously before you learn the material you will be unable to answer these questions but as the weeks go on you will have a better and better idea of how to tackle them.

By being familiar with the types of questions that you are likely to be asked in your examinations you will be able to listen more actively in your lectures, and as the lecture course progresses you will recognize material in your lectures that is relevant to the past paper questions that you

By being familiar with the types of questions that you are likely to be asked in your examinations you will be able to listen more actively in your lectures.

have studied. Then when you look at the questions again at the weekend you will be able to begin answering some of them or improve answers that you have already begun.

Your aim should be that when you come to the end of a module you will understand what is needed to give complete answers to all of the relevant questions from the recent past papers.

Summary

I know that many of you will read the last two lessons and think: "I know that this extra work is sensible and in an ideal world I would do it all, but I can't really be bothered/I don't really have the time…" - *Don't fall into this trap!*

Even a small amount of time spent on the activities that I have described to you over the last two days would be time very well spent. It would significantly improve your overall understanding and give you a distinct advantage over students who do not study well during term-time.

I've described the activities discussed over the last two days as *voluntary study* but don't think of them as *extra work;* think of them as *streamlining your learning.* Doing these tasks regularly will dramatically improve your understanding and, in the long run, save you time and reduce your stress levels.

Try to take on board the principles of what's been covered over the last two days, which are:

- Regularly revisit and try to understand your lectures as you go along.
- Organize your notes well and file them sensibly.
- Create concise summaries of your lectures; this will help you to learn your work.
- Be familiar with past examination papers. Being familiar with past papers is *extremely* useful – they are *exactly* how you will be tested.
- Be familiar with the syllabus of each of your courses and, as you go along, try to appreciate how your lectures and other classes fit into the course as a whole.

It may seem that I have created a lot of work for you in the last two lessons but these tasks really don't take long! In *Further Reading IV: Fitting it all in,* we consider just how much time is required to complete them.

Suggested Further Reading

To complement today's lesson, you may wish to read:

Further Reading IV: Fitting it all in

Day 6

Final Revision: a five-week plan

Introduction

The few weeks leading up to your exams can be quite scary, but you can help control these nerves by organizing your final revision well and by working to a timetable.

The few weeks leading up to your exams can be quite scary, but you can help control these nerves by organizing your final revision well and by working to a timetable.

I suggest that you spend around *five weeks* on final revision. If you spend much more than this then your revision period could overlap with your lectures, and it's difficult to see the course as a whole if you haven't finished it. Providing that you practice good term time study techniques, as previously discussed, then five weeks of final revision should be fine.

In their final revision many students simply sit and read through their notes over and over again in the hope that the information will stick. This is a very *passive, unimaginative,* and *ineffective* way of revising, likely to make you very bored and maybe even depressed.

Today, I am going to describe to you an example of a five-week revision timetable that, should you choose to follow it, will help to ensure that your final revision is *active, varied,* and *effective.*

In this example let's imagine that you have six lecture courses to revise. So that you don't risk running out of time, it's a good idea to revise each of your courses over the whole of the revision period. So for each of the five weeks of your final revision you could revise course one every Monday, course two every Tuesday, course three every Wednesday, and so on.

It is important that you take one day off each week and do something that you really enjoy. Looking forward to your day off (and thinking of it as a reward for working hard) will help you to maintain enthusiasm and motivation during the week.

Week 1

In week 1 create *summary sheets* for each of your courses. So on Monday you would make a summary sheet of course one, on Tuesday a summary sheet of course two, Wednesday a summary sheet of course three, and so on.

Take a large sheet of paper, A3 or

**Week 1:
Create summary
sheets for each
of your courses.**

larger, and using your study cards and lecture notes try to summarize the whole lecture course on this single sheet of paper. Take your time over this as it will be extremely useful in the upcoming weeks when you test yourself from memory. Your completed summary sheet could look like one large spider diagram in which you can visualize the course as a whole and see how each of the topics interrelate.

Each of the points on your summary sheet acts as a *memory prompter*. Your aim over the coming weeks is to be able to look at each of these points and expand upon them from memory. Each point on the summary sheet will prompt you to visualize a certain study card or a table/a diagram/a definition/a list/an equation/a derivation or chunk of text etc. from your lecture notes.

Once you're happy with your summary sheet, spend the rest of the day memorizing your study cards and summary sheet and learning things by heart.

Creating summary sheets for each of your courses and spending time memorizing them means that by the end of your first week you will have a broad understanding of each of your courses and you will be well on the way to committing the information to memory.

Week 2

Each day of week 2 *test yourself from memory*.

Place your summary sheet in front of you and look through all of the topics and headings

**Week 2:
Test yourself from
memory.**

and test yourself by writing things out from memory. Prepare diagrams from memory, write lists from memory, write definitions and equations and chemical reactions, write facts and figures, and chunks of text, all from memory. Whenever you get stuck or you want to check that you have remembered something correctly, refer to your study cards and lecture notes. You may find yourself referring to your study cards and notes quite often, however, as you repeat this process over the coming weeks, you will find yourself referring to your study cards and notes less and less frequently.

To further test your recall and understanding, spend some time solving relevant problems from your textbooks during week 2. In addition, go back over the topics discussed in your tutorials and seminars and attempt any relevant questions.

Week 3

Spend each day of week 3 *predicting examination questions*. Most students try to guess which questions are likely to be included in their examinations. This can be a useful exercise particular if you haven't studied well throughout the term.

Week 3: Predict examination questions.

For those students who have studied well throughout the term, considering past papers and trying to predict possible examination questions is still a very valuable revision exercise.

A word of caution though: you don't want to be going into an exam *hoping* that certain topics will be tested because they are the only ones that you have studied! By studying well throughout the term, maintaining a keen and active mind in your classes, and revising all aspects of the course then you should feel confident that you could attempt a question on any of the topics covered in the course.

Even the most diligent students can benefit from spending time considering which areas are *likely* to be examined.

Here are two approaches that you can take when trying to predict possible examination questions:

Firstly

Check through your notes and look for areas/topics that your lecturer drew particular attention to. If your lecturer focused on a specific topic and devoted a lot of time to discussing it then this can be a strong indicator that it will be examined.

Secondly

Look carefully at the examination papers for the last two or three years; look for questions that are frequently asked. Many examiners have certain topics that they set a question on every year. Take care when using this approach because if a certain aspect of the course is examined every year it is unlikely that you will have *exactly* the same question in your exam as has been set previously. You may get a question that relates to the same topic, but it is unlikely to be identical. It is therefore a useful exercise to write out a number of variations of these questions: analyze, define, explain, describe, compare etc. Then, for each of the questions in your list prepare a *plan* of the answer that you would give if you were faced with this question in your exam (often in revision it is sufficient to write a plan of your answer as opposed to spending time writing the answer out in full. This allows you to consider a large range of topics in a short space of time).

As we discussed in yesterday's lesson, take care when looking at past examination papers to ensure that they are relevant. You don't want to waste time looking at papers which were set when the syllabus was different or which were set by a different examiner. If your lecturer (who is usually the person who writes the examination paper) has changed in the last couple of years or if the syllabus has recently changed then this may mean that there are no (or very few) relevant past papers for a particular course. In this case your lecturer should be able to provide you with at least one specimen paper or a list of specimen questions for you to consider.

Once you have identified areas which are frequently examined spend some time reading selected passages from textbooks on these areas.

Spend whatever time you have left each day studying your summary sheet and memorizing your study cards.

Week 4

Each day of week 4 set yourself at least one mock exam paper and try to complete it/them under examination conditions. By this I mean try to complete each paper in the time that would be available to you in your exam, without referring to your notes or study aids.

**Week 4:
Each day of week 4
set yourself at least
one mock exam.**

When preparing a mock exam include questions from actual

past papers and questions that you have written yourself. When preparing questions yourself you can use past paper questions for inspiration. You could also ask a friend, who is on the same course, to create some questions for you and you could do the same for them in return.

Completing answers to suitable questions under examination conditions (i.e. without your notes and in the time that would be available to you in your exam) is excellent exam preparation.

Once again, spend whatever time you have left each day studying your summary sheet and memorizing your study cards.

Week 5

As with week 4, each day of this final week set yourself at least one mock exam, and once again spend whatever time you have left each day studying your summary sheet

**Week 5:
Each day of this final week set yourself at least one mock exam.**

and memorizing your study cards. Pay particular attention to topics that you think are *likely* to be examined and read around these areas from suitable textbooks.

Examination day

Ensure that you take all of the appropriate materials with you to your exam; sharpened pencils, a pencil sharpener, pens, a ruler, pencil erasers, a calculator, and any other items that you are likely to need/are allowed to use.

Examination centers should always have a large visible clock so that you can monitor the time during your exam, but it's often a good idea to take a watch with you or a small (silent) clock. In an exam, time management is crucial.

By following the study techniques that I have described to you, throughout the term and in the weeks leading up to your exams, then on the day of your exam you should not feel worried or stressed. Imagine how **Imagine how an athlete feels just before a race...; that is how you should feel before an exam.** an athlete feels just before a race; having put in months and months of training he would feel full of energy, he would be pumped with adrenaline, he would feel ready for action, ready to perform, and keen to show what he is capable of! That is how you should feel before an exam.

Summary

- Take control of your final revision by making a timetable and sticking to it.
- Maintain your motivation and enthusiasm over the revision period by taking one day off each week and doing something that you really enjoy.
- Revise each module over the whole revision period. By doing this you can be confident that you will not run out of time and therefore will not have to rush one or more of your modules at the end of the revision period.

In order to *learn, understand,* and *remember* information you must go over it many times and approach the information from different angles. The example revision timetable that I have described to you today ensures that you do both of these things.

I hope that today's lesson has helped to take some of the fear out of final revision for you! The key is: *be organized.*

Suggested Further Reading

To complement today's lesson, you may wish to read:

Further Reading V: Examinations

(Now that you've come to the end of this six day course, why not send me some feedback? Take a look at Part Four of this book (p.127-9) to find out how.)

Part Two

Further Reading

Further Reading I

The Study Session

Introduction

On Day 1 we said that you are studying whenever you are *actively trying to learn.*

From this statement you are studying:

- when you are in your classes and when you tackle defined homework - *we defined these aspects of study as* **compulsory** *study,*

    and,

- when you are revisiting and organizing your lecture notes; reading recommended texts; preparing summaries of your notes; considering past examination papers; and preparing for your classes etc. - *we defined these aspects of study as* **voluntary** *study.*

This further reading lesson is devoted to discussing how best to tackle your *private* study sessions (by this I mean the time you spend studying outside of your classes).

Your study area

When you sit down outside of classes to work on a piece of defined homework or to undertake some voluntary study consider the following:

Work somewhere quiet where you are not likely to be distracted or interrupted. This could be in the library or at a desk in your room. Take some time today to arrange and organize the study area in your room so that it is a pleasant place to be. Ensure that all of your materials and books are close to hand and ensure

Work somewhere quiet where you are not likely to be distracted or interrupted.

that the area is comfortable and well-lit. *These things are important*; if your study environment is well organized and orderly it helps lift your spirits and helps you think more clearly. If you are surrounded by clutter and chaos you will not want to be there, and the work you do there will not do you justice - *get this sorted today and keep it this way*.

Many of you will be living in the college dormitory or perhaps in a shared house or flat. These places can be noisy and distracting. Also, although the college library is designed to be a quiet place to study, this is not always the case. You are likely to find people from your course in the library and they may be a distraction to you, they may even want to talk with you. However, if you make use of unsociable hours to study (as we discussed on Day 2), such as in the morning before your classes begin, then you are likely to find that the library and where you live will be fairly quiet.

You may also consider making use of a library that does not directly cater for your department (if possible). For example if you are a Science student consider going to the Arts Library to study or the local public library; you are less likely to be distracted by people that you know there.

Also, be *creative* in your approach to your study tasks - some study objectives can be tackled in different ways. For example, consider recording yourself reading aloud some of your notes using a voice recorder which you can then listen to while you're jogging or taking a walk, or when you're driving or taking the bus. It is not uncommon for a student to travel for thirty minutes or so each morning to get into college and then the same in the evening. This time could be used to listen to some prerecorded course material.

At the start of the study session

On Day 2 we talked about scheduling your study sessions one day in advance. This means that when you begin a study session you will have a good idea of what you wish to achieve in the session and it will be written in your notebook - this is your *study objective*.

Start each study session on time and, on the desk in front of you, only have the books and materials that are required for the task at hand. At the start of the study session read your study objective carefully and think about what you are aiming to achieve.

I recommend that you turn to a clean page in your notebook and take a minute or so to clearly detail your study objective/s for the session (don't worry about using up lots of pages in your notebook; notebooks are dirt cheap in comparison to the cost of your course!). This step can

At the start of your study session read your study objective carefully and think about what you are aiming to achieve.

act as a *catalyst* towards an effective study session; simply by articulating your objectives in writing will help focus your thoughts and prepare your mind for the task ahead.

During the study session

Throughout the session, refer to your study objective/s so that you don't lose track of what you plan to achieve and so you remain totally focused.

After twenty minutes or so working on a task you are likely to feel your mind beginning to wander. *Do not try to carry on regardless*; it is better to pause for a couple of minutes. During this break think about something completely different. Think about something that you are looking forward to; something that will give you a buzz. Think about the reward that you will give yourself for achieving the task that you are working on. I call this a *micro-break*. After this short break return to your task. *This technique works.* It will help you to maintain attention and enthusiasm throughout the study session.

At the end of the study session

As I've said many times before: each session should be roughly between 30 minutes and an hour. It is difficult to concentrate on the same task for much longer than this.

After this time, re-read your study objective/s for the session to check that you have achieved what you set out to. Then, if you have another session planned, take a short break before moving onto the new task. Again, only have in front of you the things that are required for this new task. In order to maintain enthusiasm and interest, successive tasks should be *different kinds of activity*: revisit, read, prepare, write, think, check, etc.

In order to maintain enthusiasm and interest successive tasks should be *different kinds of activity*...

When you have finished your scheduled tasks, clear your desk and consider what you have achieved. Have you achieved what you set out to do?

Dealing with particularly difficult tasks

Technique 1

There will be times when you have a study session listed in your notebook which you know you are not going to enjoy. You may find yourself trying to push this task to the back of your mind. If you do this then the task can get blown out of proportion and it can build into something frightening.

As soon as you begin feeling this way about a study task, schedule a *five-minute study session* when you'll sit down and consider how to tackle the task. This technique helps you to overcome the fear that you have associated with the task, and once you begin to develop a strategy for dealing with it you will begin to take control over it which will dramatically reduce your stress.

Technique 2

When you sit down to tackle a particularly tedious or stressful study task it can be difficult to get your mind going - it can feel as though your mind is stubbornly refusing to cooperate! One way of dealing with such tasks is to work for just a couple of minutes then take a micro-break (i.e. pause for a minute or two and think about something else; something that will lift your spirits), then work for a couple of minutes more then take another micro-break, keep going like this until you get warmed up. These frequent micro-breaks at the beginning of the study session can help *kick-start your brain into action*. By using this technique you will soon get into the flow of it, and you'll have the task completed before you know it!

Summary

The importance of having a well organized, quiet, pleasant study area to do your work cannot be overemphasized. *Get this sorted today and keep it this way!*

Your private study should not seem like a chore. It should not be something that you dread doing. Develop a more positive attitude and be organized. Take control of your study time by having clearly defined study objectives for each and every session.

By following the advice that I have given to you in this lesson, your private study sessions should become more effective and you will be able to tackle even difficult tasks with confidence and get your work done in less time.

Further Reading II

Dealing with Coursework

Introduction

Some of your private study time will be taken up dealing with defined homework or coursework such as writing up a practical session, or tackling an essay or assignment that has been set. These pieces of work are usually assessed and will count towards your final grade.

Be organized

As we have discussed previously, the key to dealing with any large task is to break the task down into smaller, defined, sub tasks that you can deal with one at a time.

The key to dealing with any large task is to break the task down into smaller, defined, sub tasks.

I'll re-emphasize this important principle here:

Lets consider how you might approach an assignment that has been set. This is a list of individual sub tasks that you could create in order to deal with this task.

- Think about the assignment and prepare notes of ideas and information that should be included in your answer*.
- Do some background reading to get additional ideas.
- Prepare an outline/plan for your answer.
- Write your answer.
- Check your work.

This positive approach to your studies means that you are in control. This will reduce your stress and improve your confidence.

*Whenever you are given an assignment spend time *carefully considering what is required* before you begin to tackle it. Your assessor will usually have a mark scheme (a list of points that he/she wishes to see in your assignment for which you will be awarded marks). Try to figure out *exactly* what you think the assessor wants to see.

Present your work well

The person marking your work is a human being (despite any rumors to the contrary!), and he/she will have dozens of assignments/ practical write-ups to grade.

It is in your interests to present your work well to allow for ease and speed of marking.

Therefore it is in your interests to present your work well to allow for ease and speed of marking. If your assignment is clumsy and/or illegible and your assessor has to search for the information that is required then the mark that you receive will often be affected.

Therefore,

When completing defined homework:

- Use distinct and effective paragraphing.
- Arrange your paragraphs/sections in an appropriate and logical order.
- Use concise sentences that convey your point exactly.
- Ensure that each section of your assignment is clearly distinguished.
- If you hand-write your composition, ensure your writing is legible.
- Cite all the references used in your composition carefully; there are definitive rules on how to do this.
- Number and label your tables and figures, and make sure they are referred to at least once in the text.
- Take out any superfluous words, sentences, and paragraphs that could distract the reader from what you are trying to say.
- Stick within the word/page limit. If you have a limit of say 1000 words and you write 1200 words then some assessors will only mark the first 1000 words and they will give you no credit for anything written beyond that point.

This list may seem daunting, but look upon improving your presentation skills as a *challenge*. Getting these things right takes practice, but if you master them early, the time you spend dealing with defined homework/coursework will become much easier (you might even begin to enjoy it - just as you enjoy doing anything that you are good at).

One final point to remember on this subject: although presentation *is* important it is not a *substitute* for content. There is no point in submitting a beautifully presented assignment if the content does not answer the question set!

Learn from the assessors remarks

When you get back a piece of work that has been marked, consider carefully any comments or corrections that the assessor has made. You will probably be eager to know the mark that you have been awarded and therefore you may pay little attention to any feedback. Develop a better attitude. Any comments that the assessor has written are *very valuable* and if you take the time to consider them then you can improve the grade you receive for your next piece of work.

Final year project

Many degree schemes require the student to undertake a special investigation or prepare a special composition in their final year; this is often simply referred to as *the final year project*. This is the largest assessed composition that you will face. When the time comes you will receive guidance from your tutors on how best to approach this task, but if you take on board and practice the principles that I have described here then you will be well prepared when it comes to dealing with your final year project.

Summary

The ability to communicate concisely and effectively through writing is an essential skill, so be organized in your approach to your defined homework and constantly strive to improve the presentation of your compositions.

Further Reading III

Writing Essays

Introduction

The ability to communicate concisely and effectively through writing is an essential skill. Many students find writing essays difficult, but there are some simple rules that you can follow to help you, and with practice your confidence will soon grow.

In this lesson we will be thinking about how to tackle an essay *outside* of an examination. This could be an essay that is set for coursework or an essay from a past examination paper that you are attempting as part of your private study. In *Further Reading V: Examinations* we will discuss attempting essay questions in an examination.

We can all improve our writing skills. An effective way of doing this is to consider the work of other writers. You can do this by studying articles in good newspapers, and articles in magazines and journals that are relevant to your course. As always, keep a keen mind and read actively and critically. Pay particular attention to the author's use of language and notice how the article is structured.

On occasion, when you're reading something by a talented author you will find yourself reading a passage over and over, not necessarily because the topic is particularly interesting, but because the passage is written so well. It is always impressive to find a piece of writing where a difficult concept is expressed *simply* and *clearly*.

Essay writing is one of the principle ways in which you are examined and your ability to write essays plays a huge part in determining your grade, yet many students do not practice essay writing.

When writing an essay there are four stages you should consider; *Think, Plan, Write, and Check.*

There are simple rules that you can follow to help you with your compositions. When writing an essay there are four stages you should consider; *Think, Plan, Write, and Check.*

Think

Before you tackle an essay question, take some time to carefully consider what is required.

When thinking about the question, consider every word and phrase to make sure that you understand *exactly* what the assessor wants to know, and for indications of how you should present your answer.

You may find it helpful to read the question aloud to yourself. Simply by verbalizing a question out loud, as opposed to merely thinking the words, can sometimes

When thinking about the question, consider every word and phrase to make sure that you understand *exactly* what the assessor wants to know.

cause you to think of the question in a different way.

Plan

When you are *sure* you know what the question means you must plan your answer.

Lets consider how to do this:

- Firstly, list all of the main points that you wish to include in your answer. Each of these will form a paragraph in your essay.
- Below these headings you should then add further notes as you expand upon these points with relevant information, examples, and ideas that you wish to include.
- Then, decide upon an effective order for your paragraphs.
- Finally you must consider how your essay is to be introduced and how it is to be drawn to a conclusion.

With your plan complete look again at the question to confirm that it provides the basis for a good answer.

Write

When you write your essay, work to your plan. By doing this your answer should be well balanced and well organized.

Your essay should be clear, concise, and orderly and the information it contains must be relevant, accurate, and complete.

Your essay should be clear, concise, and orderly and the information it contains must be relevant, accurate, and complete.

Use the first paragraph to introduce the subject. In the first paragraph try to make it clear that you understand the question. The best way to do this is to use this first paragraph to get across the essence of your answer using words from the question appropriately.

In each of the subsequent paragraphs deal with one distinct topic. Use the first sentence of each paragraph to indicate what the paragraph is about. In each paragraph only include relevant information (information that will score you marks), and try to express your thoughts as clearly and simply as you can.

By making your paragraphs distinct, effective, and economical your essay will be easier to mark; the assessor will be grateful for this.

Your sentences should be concise, considered, and contain only relevant information. It is often best to keep your sentences short; often a sentence will convey a single thought. Try not to use more words than is necessary to convey your meaning precisely.

When completing an essay assignment as a piece of coursework you may wish to end your essay with a summary in which the main points made in your essay are restated. Be aware, however, that if you present the same information more than once you are unlikely to be awarded the marks more than once! Instead of a summary, it is usually more appropriate to use the final paragraph of your essay to make any necessary conclusions. Similarly, it is not usually necessary to convey the same information in the form of both words and a diagram.

Check your essay

If your work is handwritten make sure that every word is legible. If the assessor can't read something then he/she cannot give you any marks for it! Illegibility also creates an unfavorable impression. If (like myself) your handwriting isn't great then try to improve it. In an exam especially, legibility and speed of writing are essential.

Check that you have not exceeded the word/page limit for the essay. This is important. Many assessors will stop reading at the set limit and therefore you will not gain any credit for anything written beyond it.

Once you have written your essay, re-read the question and consider if there is anything *more* that could be added to your essay. Is there something that you have missed out?

Conversely, is there anything in your essay that is irrelevant; something that will not score you any marks? If so, consider taking it out. Even if the information is correct, if it is not relevant you will not be given any credit for it (worse still, irrelevant sentences/paragraphs can distract the assessor from what you are trying to say or make your answer confusing, either of which may result in a loss of marks).

Learn from the assessor's remarks

When you get back a piece of work that has been marked, consider carefully any comments or corrections that the assessor has written. You will probably be eager to know the mark that you have been awarded and therefore you may pay little attention to any feedback. Develop a better attitude. Any comments that the assessor has written are *very valuable* and if you take the time to consider them then you can improve the grade you receive for your next piece of work.

Summary

When faced with an essay question always think carefully about *exactly* what the assessor wants to see in your answer. Once you've thought about the question, write a plan. The ability to write good essay plans is very important – *always write a plan.*

When writing your essay, ensure that your paragraphs are relevant, distinct, effective, and economical. The effective use of paragraphs may seem like a trivial or obvious skill but it is often misunderstood.

A well-composed essay that conveys relevant information and good ideas clearly and simply is often impressive and is something that you can take pride in.

A well-composed essay that conveys relevant information and good ideas clearly and simply is impressive and is something that you can take pride in.

I hope that this lesson has helped you to feel more confident about tackling essays; the rules are really quite simple once you understand them: *Think, Plan, Write, then Check.*

Further Reading IV

Fitting it all in

Introduction

On Days 4 and 5 we discussed some of the ways in which you can make good use of your free time on weekdays and on weekends during term-time. In this lesson I hope to demonstrate how you can easily fit all of these voluntary study activities into your week if you manage your time well.

Table IV.3 shows a typical timetable for a first year student studying for a science related degree. I have chosen to discuss the timetable of a science student because such students tend to have the busiest timetables in terms of the amount of time spent in classes.

In the timetable I have shown all of the *compulsory study sessions* (made up of the students' classes plus the time the student devotes to dealing with defined homework/coursework) and all of the *voluntary study sessions* undertaken in a typical week.

The time slots allocated to classes are in fixed positions (determined by the students' department). The time slots illustrated for dealing with defined homework and all aspects of voluntary study are chosen by the student; these are not in regular time slots. This example is purely to illustrate how you *could* fit in all of the studying that I suggest if you manage your time well. For the reasons given on p.19, there are many advantages to planning your study sessions just one day in advance.

To help you understand Table IV.3 let's discuss the nature of the time slots illustrated.

Compulsory study sessions

Classes

In the example timetable there are:

- Four lecture courses being taught simultaneously; lecture courses A, B, C, and D. There are two lectures each week for each of these courses.
- Two practical courses running simultaneously; Practical Course I and Practical Course II. Each practical course has one three hour session each week.
- One tutorial and one seminar each week.

Defined homework

In Table IV.3 I have illustrated how you can fit in study sessions to deal with defined homework. The timetable illustrates eight study sessions each week dedicated to dealing with defined homework (illustrated as **Defined h'work**). For a science student this will primarily involve writing up practical classes. Depending on which course you are doing the nature of your defined homework will be different; a student of history would perhaps spend these sessions completing essay assignments for example.

Voluntary study sessions

On Days 4 and 5 I suggested three voluntary study activities to be completed on weekdays and three to be completed on weekends during term-time. Tables IV.1 and IV.2, overleaf, will help you understand the terms used in Table IV.3 relating to voluntary study.

Weekdays:

suggested study task	*illustrated as:*
One *revisiting* session is timetabled for each lecture.	*Revisit lecture: course A*
One study session per lecture course per week is dedicated to *reading recommended texts*.	*Textbook: course A*
Four study sessions have been allocated to *preparing for classes*: lectures, practical sessions, and tutorials/seminars. E.g. *Prepare Lecs (A/B)* means prepare for lecture courses A and B.	*Prepare for Lecs (A/B)*

Table IV.1: weekday voluntary study tasks

Weekends:

suggested study task	*illustrated as:*
One study session is allocated on the weekend to *organizing notes*.	*organize notes*
One study session per lecture course is allocated to *creating study cards*.	*Study cards - course A*
One study session per lecture course is allocated to *considering past examination papers*.	*Past papers - course A*

Table IV.2: weekend voluntary study tasks

	Mon	Tues	Wed	Thurs	Fri	Sat	Sun
07:00 -08:00						*organize notes*	
08:00 -09:00			**Defined h'work**		**Defined h'work**		
09:00 -09:50	*Prepare for Lecs (A/B)*	**Lecture: course A**	*Textbook: course B*		*Textbook: course C*	*Study cards - course A*	
10:00 -10:50	**Lecture: course A**	**Tutorial**	**Lecture: course B**	**Seminar**	*Prac II Write-up*	*Past papers - course A*	
Morning Break							
11:10 -12:00	**Lecture: course B**	*Revisit lecture: course A*	*Revisit lecture: course B*	**Lecture: course D**	**Lecture: course D**	*Study cards - course B*	*Study cards - course C*
12:10 -13:00	*Revisit lecture: course A*	*Prepare for Lecs (C/D)*	**Lecture: course C**	*Revisit lecture: course D*	*Revisit lecture: course D*	*Past papers - course B*	*Past papers - course C*
Lunch							
14:10 -15:00	*Revisit lecture: course B*	**Practical Session I**	**Defined h'work**	**Practical Session II**	**Lecture: course C**		*Study cards - course D*
15:10 -16:00	*Textbook: course A*	**Practical Session I**		**Practical Session II**	*Revisit lecture: course C*		*Past papers - course D*
16:10 -17:00					*Textbook: course D*		
17:00 -18:00	*Prepare for practicals*	**Defined h'work**		**Defined h'work**			
18:00 -19:00					*Prepare for tut/sem*		
19:00 -20:00		**Defined h'work**	*Revisit lecture: course C*	**Defined h'work**			

Table IV.3: typical 1st year timetable for a student of science, showing compulsory study (**bold**) and voluntary study (*italics*). For further explanation see text plus Tables IV.1 and IV.2. **Note**: Each time slot in Table IV.3 is one hour long, whereas many of the tasks could take as little as 30 minutes.

Summary

I hope that this example has illustrated that if you organize your study time well and make good use of your free periods during the day then all of the voluntary study sessions that I have suggested can easily be fitted into your week.

I also hope that the example makes it obvious that by using your time well, you can free up large chunks of your weekday evenings and weekends to use as you wish.

By using your time well, you can free up large chunks of your weekday evenings and weekends to use as you wish.

Finally, working hard is obviously important but remember to reward yourself! So, when you've completed your study tasks, go out and have fun, play sport, spend time with your friends, etc. - these things are vital for the development of a healthy body and mind.

Further Reading V

Examinations

Before the Exam

As soon as the examination timetable becomes available, CAREFULLY note the times and locations of all of your exams. You may find that some of your exams will take place in locations which are unfamiliar to you. It's vital, therefore, that you find out exactly where the exam will take place, how to get there, and how long it will take you to travel there. It may sound over the top, but it's often a good idea to *rehearse* beforehand the journey to the examination venue. The last thing you want is to be wandering the streets in a blind panic looking for the examination center when you should already be there - as horrible as this sounds, it happens every year!

As soon as the examination timetable becomes available CAREFULLY note the times and locations of all your exams.

The last few lectures of the course

You cannot afford to miss the last few lectures of a course. In these lectures, pay particular attention to what the lecturer *emphasizes*. Often, during these sessions, the lecturer will give you hints as to what may be included in the exam, so concentrate and try to pick these hints up!

The night before the exam

If you feel you need to, look over your summary sheets and study cards one last time, but be aware that too much studying the night before an exam can make you stressed and may not be very productive. It's better to focus on relaxing and getting a good night's sleep. If you are having trouble relaxing then try going for a walk. This will help clear your mind and relax your body. Then try to get an early night. This way you will be rested and in the best state of mind for your exam. If the exam is in the morning then remember to set your alarm clock and allow yourself plenty of time to have breakfast, get yourself ready, and make your way to the examination center.

The day of the exam

Bring all of the appropriate materials with you to the exam: sharpened pencils, a pencil sharpener, pens, a ruler, pencil erasers, a calculator, and any other items that you will need and that you are allowed to use. Examination centers should always have a large visible clock so that you can monitor the time during the exam, but it's often a good idea to take a watch with you or a small (silent) clock. In an exam, time management is crucial.

I know that you will be feeling nervous, but try to eat something before your exam to help keep your energy levels up and so that you don't get distracted in your exam by feeling hungry.

Arrive at the examination venue with plenty of time to spare, but bear in mind that it's not usually a good idea to discuss notes with anyone immediately before an exam. There will be students saying things like *I haven't done any revision for this exam. I'm bound to fail!* Also, students may wish to discuss their theories about which questions are going to come up. You may also find some fellow students trying to ask you last minute questions in an attempt to supplement their lack of studying. Try to stay away from these discussions because they are likely to be distracting and confusing.

The Exam

Before you start your exam, close your eyes and take a few deep breaths to help control your nerves. Remember however, that you are trying to compose yourself - not put yourself to sleep; you should feel alert and ready for action!

READ ALL INSTRUCTIONS VERY CAREFULLY. You should be very familiar with the structure of the paper from your work with past papers, but it is still essential that you read the instructions carefully and consider what is required.

READ ALL INSTRUCTIONS VERY CAREFULLY.

Also, listen for any announcements. Make sure that you understand all of the instructions and announcements completely before attempting the exam. If you have any questions about the instructions or the announcements then make sure that you ask to have them clarified for you.

Look at both sides of each page (in particular look carefully at the front and *back* of the last page) in order to make sure that you see *all* of the questions. You don't want to leave your exam and have a friend ask for example, "What did you think of question 7?" and you think, "There wasn't a question 7!" because you didn't see it! This is a common scenario, so make sure that you take a good look at every page of the examination paper and identify all of the questions before you start.

The way in which an examination paper is structured will vary from subject to subject as will the types of questions that are asked. Typically however, an examination paper has a section of short questions followed by a section where you have a choice of longer (usually essay type) questions. Allocate time for each section of the exam paper in relation to how many marks each section is worth, and keep an eye on the time throughout the exam in order to spend the appropriate length of time on each section.

Allocate time for each section of the exam paper in relation to how many marks each section is worth.

The short question section

Attempt the questions that you are most confident/ comfortable with first. This will help you to relax and help you to get into a positive frame of mind. If you are required to write your answers in an answer booklet (as opposed to writing directly onto the question paper) then ensure that each answer is clearly numbered so that the assessor can easily see which answer relates to which question. Once you have gone through the whole of the section and answered all of the questions that you are confident with, you can return to the beginning and attempt the questions you were less sure of. You are likely to find these questions, which initially seemed difficult, easier to attempt on the second reading. If you are still struggling with one or two of the questions then do not dwell on them. You do not want to get stuck on one item as this can be very frustrating which may have a negative effect upon the rest of the exam. You can always return to these questions later.

When dealing with questions that require a calculation (or a derivation) ensure that you show all of the stages necessary to reach the answer. If you just write the final answer, even if it is correct, you will not be given all of the available marks because you have not shown the workings of your calculation. The examiner's mark scheme will often include the key elements of the calculation, and marks will be awarded for each of these key elements given in your answer. Therefore, even if your final answer is *wrong*, you can score marks for the parts of your workings which are correct.

Essay questions

When you have a choice of essay questions in an examination, read all of the questions carefully and consider what is required for each answer before deciding which you can answer best.

In *Further Reading III: Writing Essays* I suggested that when you tackle an essay question you should: *think, plan, write,* and then *check.* Here we will consider essay writing under examination conditions. Typically, in an exam you will have about 35 minutes to complete all of these stages. Use this time wisely and effectively (see Table V.1):

Activity	Time needed (approx.)
Thinking and planning	5 minutes
Writing your answer	25 minutes
Checking your work	5 minutes

Table V.1: approx. time required for the stages necessary when attempting an essay question in an exam.

Think:

Before you tackle an essay question in an exam take some time to carefully consider exactly what is required before you plan your answer.

Quietly mouthing the question to yourself can be very beneficial. Verbalizing the question, as opposed to merely thinking the words in your head, can sometimes cause you to think of the question in a different way.

Consider every word and phrase in the question to make sure that you understand *exactly* what the examiner wants to know and for indications of the way you should present your answer.

It's important that you answer *precisely* the question asked and not a slightly different question that you would prefer! If your knowledge is insufficient to answer precisely the question asked then don't simply right down everything that you know in an attempt to make it look like a good answer! Even if the information that you give in your answer is correct, if it's not what is asked for then you cannot score any marks for it. Think about what you do know then only give information that is relevant to the question asked.

Plan:

When you are sure that you know what the question means you must plan your answer. When preparing your plan bear in mind that if the question is divided into several parts and each part has a number of marks allocated to it then this can be an indicator of how much you should write for each part. For example, if one part of the question has *three* marks allocated to it then there are likely to be *three* statements, or lines of reasoning, that the examiner wishes to see in your answer.

Preparing a plan:

- Firstly, note down all of the main points that you wish to include in your answer. Each of these will form a *paragraph* in your essay.
- Below these headings you should then add further notes as you expand upon these points with relevant information, examples, and ideas that you wish to include.
- Then, consider how you are going to introduce your answer and decide upon an effective order for your paragraphs.
- Finally, you must consider how your essay is to be drawn to a conclusion.

With your plan complete, look again at the question to confirm that your plan does provide the basis for a good answer.

Write:

When you write your essay, work to your plan. By doing this your answer should be well balanced and well organized.

Your essay should be clear, concise, and orderly and the information it contains must be relevant, accurate, and complete.

Use the first paragraph to introduce the subject, and try to make it clear that you understand the question. The best way to do this is to use this first paragraph to get across the essence of your answer using words from the question appropriately.

In each of the subsequent paragraphs, deal with one distinct topic. Try to express your thoughts as clearly and as simply as you can. Use the first sentence of each paragraph to indicate what the paragraph is about. In each paragraph only include relevant information; information that will score you marks. By making your paragraphs distinct, effective, and economical your essay will be easier to mark; the assessor will be grateful for this.

Your sentences should be concise, considered, and effective containing only relevant information. Try to keep your sentences short; often a sentence will convey a single thought. Try not to use more words than is necessary to convey your meaning precisely.

Do not waste time by conveying the same information more than once, for example do not convey the same information as both words and a diagram. Also, when tackling an essay question in an exam it's not usually necessary to use the final paragraph to summarize what you have already said in the bulk of the essay. You should use the final paragraph to make any conclusions, if it is appropriate to do so.

Note: Make sure that the examiner can easily distinguish your essay plan from your actual essay. Once you have written your essay you may wish to put a neat line through your plan so that the examiner can clearly distinguish it from your answer.

Check:

Make sure that every word in your essay is legible; if the assessor can't read something he/she cannot give you any marks for it! Illegibility also creates an unfavorable impression. If (like myself) your handwriting isn't great then try to improve it. In an exam, legibility and speed of writing are essential.

Re-read the question and consider if there is anything more that could be added to your answer. Is there anything that you have missed out?

Conversely, is there anything in your essay that is irrelevant; something that will not score you any marks? If so, consider taking it out. Even if the information is correct, if it is not relevant you will not be given any credit for it (worse still, irrelevant sentences/paragraphs can distract the assessor from what you are trying to say or make your answer confusing, either of which may result in a loss of marks).

Use your time well and do not rush through an exam. No extra marks are awarded for finishing first! If at all possible leave time at the end of your exam to check through all of your answers again.

After the exam

When your exam is finished, make some time to reward yourself in some way - you've earned it, and take some time to rest before you turn your attention to any other exams that you may have.

Part Three

Supplemental

Supplementary Lesson I

Motivation and Stress

Motivation

- When your get up and go has got up and gone.

Everyone's energy and enthusiasm for study comes in waves; you will experience peaks and troughs. You will have days when studying is enjoyable and productive, and a successful study session will give you a real sense of achievement. On other days studying will feel depressing; you may find yourself sitting at your desk staring blankly at your work wishing you were somewhere else, anywhere else! *We all have days like this.*

You may find yourself sitting at your desk staring blankly at your work wishing you were somewhere else, anywhere else! *We all have days like this.*

In the first half of this lesson I will suggest some strategies for coping with these ups and downs. We will have discussed some of this advice in previous chapters but there's no harm in going over it again.

- Always have a well-defined study objective for each study session so that you know exactly what you have to do. Then, once the task is complete you will feel a sense of achievement.
- When scheduling your work for the following day it's a good idea to organize it so that successive tasks are different kinds of activity: solve, plan, check, make notes on, review, write, read, etc.; this keeps your study periods varied and more interesting.
- Whenever you wish to learn or memorize something in your private study, devote several short study periods to the task rather than a single long one.
- When your enthusiasm is low choose a less challenging study objective from your study list, something quick and easy.
- Do not schedule more study tasks in an evening than you are likely to be able to achieve. If day after day you fail to reach the targets that you set for yourself then you will quickly become disheartened. In fact, it can be *more* productive to schedule yourself fewer study tasks than you know you will be able to achieve; by not working to your maximum every day will help you to maintain your enthusiasm for longer.
- If you are about to start studying (or are in the middle of a study session) and your friends call and ask you to go out, remember that sometimes it is the *right* decision to go out with your friends. If you constantly say to your friends that you are staying in to study then one day they'll stop calling.
- There will be times when you have a study session listed in your notebook which you know you are not going to enjoy. You may find yourself trying to push

this task to the back of your mind. If you do this then the task can get blown out of proportion and build into something frightening. As soon as you begin feeling this way, schedule a *five-minute study session* where you'll sit down and consider how to tackle the task. This technique helps you to overcome the fear that you have associated with the task, and once you begin to develop a strategy for dealing with it you will begin to take control over it, which will dramatically reduce your stress.

- If you have a task to do that you know you are avoiding then put the relevant papers or books in a visible place in your room. This will make it harder for you to ignore the task and it will make you get around to dealing with it more quickly. Don't hide from it!

- If you have a particularly difficult or less enjoyable study task to complete then schedule it for a time when you know that you will be at your best. This is usually during the hours of daylight and/or when you are least likely to be interrupted.

- Reward yourself! If you treat the things that you enjoy doing as rewards for working hard then you'll enjoy them more and it will help maintain your enthusiasm for studying.

- After twenty minutes or so working on a task you are likely to feel your mind beginning to wander. *Do not try to carry on regardless;* it is better to pause for a couple of minutes. During this break think about something completely different. Think about something that you are looking forward to; something that will give you a buzz. Think about the reward that you will give yourself for achieving the task that you are working on. I call this a *micro-break*. After this short break return to your task. *This technique works.* It will help you to maintain attention and enthusiasm throughout the study session.

- When you sit down to tackle a particularly tedious or stressful study task it can be difficult to get your mind going - it can feel as though your mind is stubbornly refusing to cooperate! One way of dealing with such tasks is to work for just a couple of minutes then take a micro-break (i.e. pause for a minute or two and think about something else; something that will lift your spirits), then work for a couple of minutes more then take another micro-break. Keep going like this until you get warmed up. These frequent micro-breaks at the beginning of the study session can help *kick-start your brain into action*. By using this technique you will soon get into the flow of it, and you'll have the task completed before you know it!

- Finally (you'll like this one), if you find that none of the above advice is working and you find yourself skipping study sessions and you feel that your heart isn't in it, then don't beat yourself up, just recognize that you're in a temporary slump and go and do something fun! Your aim then is to get out of this slump as quickly as you can by steadily rebuilding your study time back to its normal level. This attitude will help you to keep the slumps short and less stressful because you understand what is happening and you take control.

Stress

Perceiving Stress

Stress is a condition of uncertainty; you experience it when you have a lack of control over a situation. It is also caused by the fear of the unknown.

Stress is *normal;* it's how you *perceive* it that makes the difference; you can choose to deal with it *positively* or *negatively*.

Stress is *normal;* it's how you *perceive* it that makes the difference; you can choose to deal with it *positively* or *negatively*.

Let's consider an example:
It's just a few weeks until Gabriel's exams and he is experiencing stress. This stress is perfectly normal. He is stressed because:

- His degree is important to him and he wants to do well,
- His term time studying hasn't been great,
- He (obviously) does not know what the questions in the exam will be,
- He doesn't know whether or not he will be able to perform well on the day of the exam.

Gabriel now has a choice:
He can choose to use the stress that he is feeling in a *positive* way or in a *negative* way; he can either face his anxieties (*fight*) or run away from the situation (*flight*).

Positive (fight)

There are many people who thrive on stress, and many jobs have a large element of stress. Often, the people who work in these environments say that the

When stress is perceived in a positive way then it can act as a *motivator*.

stress gives them a buzz, an adrenaline rush, which motivates them and pushes them on to achieve; *they enjoy the stress!* If Gabriel uses his stress positively then it gives him energy and provides him with *motivation*. He can use it to motivate himself to learn about (and put into practice) effective study and revision techniques to ensure that he will be well prepared for whatever questions come up in the exams. He can also practice stress management techniques so he can be confident that on the day of the exam he will not panic and that he will do himself justice. When stress is perceived in a positive way then it can act as a *motivator*.

Negative (flight)

If Gabriel perceives the stress in a negative way he may try to ignore the stress. He may try to push it to the back of his mind without addressing its causes. If he does this then as time goes on it will become harder and harder for him to face his anxieties and he will become more and more anxious and upset and even ill. Negative stress (sometimes called *distress*) can lead to physical and mental *laziness*.

Negative stress (sometimes called *distress*) can lead to physical and mental *laziness*.

Coping with stress

"Maturity of the mind is the increased capacity to endure uncertainty."
                                                                - John Finlay

Identifying what is causing your stress can be a difficult task but it is the first step towards dealing with it.

Many things will contribute to your stress such as leaving home for the first time, coping financially, dealing with examinations, juggling studying and your social life, working a part time job, etc.

Taking charge of a situation and being in control will lessen the negative stress that you feel.

The best way to reduce stress is to:

1. *Acknowledge that you are stressed* - the sooner you are aware of feeling stress the sooner you can begin to deal with it.
2. *Identify the cause/s* - this is not always straightforward. You have to look within yourself and do some honest self-exploration.
3. *Address the cause/s* – confront, head on, the cause/s of your stress.

Writing is a very powerful tool when looking within yourself. Simply by identifying what is stressing you and writing it down will greatly diminish your stress. By writing down the causes of your stress you are, if you like, *making your enemies visible*. You can then look at each of the causes one at a time and devise strategies to defeat them or minimize their impact.

A very effective way of doing this is by keeping a diary/journal, which you use to explore the things that are stressing you and to come up with suggestions and steps to put them right. You don't have to write every night, only when you feel you need to. This is something that I do regularly. Whenever I'm feeling confused or stressed about something, it could be work related or something in my personal life, then I write about it in my diary. I take my time and identify exactly what is causing these feelings of uncertainty/stress and then I try to come up with ways to combat or resolve these issues. By the time I've finished writing I always feel a lot better because I have taken control of the situation. It helps me keep on top of things and helps prevent stressful situations getting out of hand.

I look at it like this: whenever I get a feeling of uncertainty/depression/distress then my subconscious is saying to me: "Something is wrong. You're not dealing with something very well." Your subconscious cannot communicate to you in words, only in feelings, and this is the way that it does it. You then need to stop and take some time to figure out exactly what is wrong and try to put it right.

By following these steps you take control and use your stress in a positive way. You use it as a *motivator* to change aspects of your life for the better.

Preventing stress

There are a number of techniques and strategies that you can use everyday to help you combat stress before it occurs as well as whilst you are experiencing it.

Exercise

> Regular exercise is a great way to relieve stress. You shouldn't look upon exercise as a chore. Develop a better attitude and find an activity that you enjoy doing.

Diet

> *You are what you eat.* This applies both physically and mentally. A good nutritious diet will help you keep a fit body and a clear mind - both of which will help you deal with the effects of stress.

Relaxation

There are many techniques that you can learn that will help you to relax, I will briefly mention two here:

- Progressive relaxation - lie down and clear your mind. Then slowly tense and relax each of your muscles in turn, working from your toes up to your head. This helps you to achieve a state of deep relaxation.
- Another popular relaxation technique involves clearing your mind and focusing on your breathing, in and out, in and out, as a means of achieving relaxation. This technique can be used almost anywhere, even in an exam.

Practicing relaxation techniques is an excellent way of reducing everyday stress. It is also an excellent aid to concentration.

Journey outside of your comfort zone

Practice doing things outside of your comfort zone, for example:

- Change the way you dress or do your hair,
- take a holiday to somewhere you've never been before,
- join a club that you're interested in,
- if you're a member of a club and nominations come up for chairperson or secretary then, if you believe you would enjoy the role, put yourself forward for nomination,
- take a different route into college,
- instead of going to the cinema go and see a play,

- take up a new sport,
- change things about your daily routine.

All of these subtle journeys outside of your comfort zone (journeys into the unknown) will be slightly stressful, but use this stress positively; enjoy the buzz and the excitement that doing something new gives you. This will help you to become acclimatized to stress in a controlled way. It will help you to develop a positive attitude to stress and help you to deal with unexpected stress.

Be prepared

When it comes to dealing with examination stress the best way to reduce your stress is to *be prepared*. If you are prepared then you should feel confident and in control.

Define your expectations – *this section is important for students who are in the last year or two of their degree. If this applies to you then think about this section carefully.*

As you progress through your course and get a better idea of what you *can* achieve and what you would *like* to achieve, ask yourself:

- What grade would I like to achieve in my degree?
- What do I expect to achieve?

I strongly believe that you should not underestimate yourself and that you should aim high. However, in order to avoid blind optimism this attitude must be tempered with *realism*. Put your emotions to one side and consider what your realistic expectations are in terms of how hard you are prepared to work and what you expect to achieve. Once you have defined these expectations you are then in a position to take control of them. This will alleviate stress and empower you.

By defining realistic expectations you will be able to devise an appropriate approach to studying that will help you to realize your goals.

Some students will define success as nothing less than achieving the highest degree classification. Others will define success as achieving a pass grade.

- What are *you* aiming for?
- What is your realistic expectation (without selling yourself short)?

These are difficult questions to answer but they are important. If you are finding that aiming for a very high class of degree is proving too much for you and is causing you a lot of stress, then you may wish to re-evaluate your expectations. If you make the decision to do this then you can adjust your studying appropriately; a person aiming for the highest degree classification will study differently to a person *consciously* aiming for a lower grade. The latter student may wish only to learn the essentials of certain courses and may accept a lower performance from himself/herself in some areas. This will free up time to concentrate on areas of the course that he/she finds more interesting and easier to learn. Making this decision can take a great weight off a student's shoulders, and he/she can still achieve a grade to be proud of.

Summary

Don't let negative stress win! Find out what is causing your stress, face up to it, be strong, and fight the causes head on.

If you take a positive view of stress then it becomes your friend. It tells you when things are not going well and that you need to do something to put them right. It even gives you the motivational energy to make positive changes.

There may be stressful elements of your life that you cannot completely eliminate. Think about how you can minimize their impact then try to make peace with them and look for any positive aspects to them.

IF YOU FEEL THAT YOU ARE NOT COPING WELL WITH ANY OF THE PRESSURES OF COLLEGE LIFE THEN SEEK HELP! THERE ARE ALWAYS PEOPLE WHO YOU CAN TALK TO, SUCH AS A FRIEND, A FAMILY MEMBER, ONE OF YOUR LECTURERS, A COLLEGE COUNSELOR, OR SOMEONE AT THE STUDENTS' UNION – THESE PEOPLE ARE THERE FOR YOU.

Supplementary Lesson II

How to Remember

Introduction

A lot of thought and planning has gone into the content and structure of this book, and in this lesson I hope to explain to you how all of the advice that I have given to you actually helps you to *learn*, *understand*, and *remember*, because after all; that's the whole point isn't it!

In order to *learn*, *understand*, and *remember* information it is best to:

- Go over it many times, and,
- Approach it in many different ways (using different senses and stimuli).

Go over and over and over your work!

Think of a specific topic that is covered in one of your college courses. If you follow all of the advice that I have given to you in this book then you will encounter this topic again and again and again as follows:

1. When you prepare for classes by doing preliminary reading,
2. When you listen actively in lectures and other classes,
3. When you actively take part in practical classes and in fieldwork,
4. When you revisit your lecture notes,
5. When you consider the course as a whole,
6. When you prepare study cards,
7. When you revisit lectures and refer back to previous lectures in the same series,
8. Each time you use your knowledge: for example when completing coursework; when you write up practical classes; when you attempt a past paper question; when you do exercises in textbooks; and in your discussions with other students,
9. When you revise your study cards and prepare summary sheets during your final revision,
10. When you test yourself and revise your work in the weeks leading up to your exams.

Thinking about your work again and again in this way helps you to understand, to see connections, and to remember. Each time you go over something it is easier to refresh your memory than the time before.

Each time you go over something it is easier to refresh your memory than the time before.

Compare this with a student who:

- does not prepare for his/her classes,
- does not keep a keen mind in lectures and simply passively transcribes what is being said,
- does not revisit his/her lectures after class, and,
- only looks at his/her notes a few weeks before the exams.

When such a student considers their lectures in the weeks leading up to the exams, it is as though they are seeing the information for the *first time*. This puts them at a massive disadvantage compared to a student who has studied well throughout the term.

Make use of different senses and stimuli to learn

We've seen how learning is aided by repetition; it is also aided by the use of different senses or stimuli.

If you follow all of the advice given to you in this book then you will learn by listening, observing, touching, reading, writing, talking, and thinking:

If you follow all of the advice given to you in this book then you will learn by listening, observing, touching, reading, writing, talking, and thinking.

Learn by Listening

- You listen and learn in lectures.
- You listen and learn in tutorials and seminars where students and tutors contribute to discussions relating to your subject.
- You listen and learn in practical and fieldwork sessions where instructions are given and phenomena

    explained.
- You listen and learn when you discuss your subject with friends.

Learn by Observing

- You observe and learn in your classes where your lecturer/tutor may draw diagrams, flow charts, and tables etc. to help convey ideas.
- You observe and learn in practical sessions and fieldwork where your skills and understanding are developed by seeing the objects, processes, and phenomena that relate to your subject.

Learn by Touching

- You touch and learn in practical sessions and fieldwork where you can manipulate the materials and equipment that relate to your subject.

Learn by Reading

- You read and learn when you revisit each of your lectures.
- You read and learn when you consider recommended textbooks.
- You read and learn when you prepare for your classes.
- You read and learn when you consider past examination papers.
- You read and learn when doing background research in order to complete defined homework.
- You read and learn when you consider the remarks that an assessor has written relating to your completed homework.

Learn by Writing

- You write and learn in lectures when you carefully select and record the main points.
- You write and learn when you revisit your work and represent your notes in a different form.
- You write and learn when you create summaries of what you have read in the recommended texts.
- You write and learn when you create study cards.
- You write and learn when you complete defined homework.
- You write and learn during your final revision when you prepare summary sheets.
- You write and learn when you attempt questions from past examination papers.

Learn by Talking

- You talk and learn when you participate in tutorials and seminars.
- You talk and learn when you ask questions in your classes.
- You talk and learn when you discuss your work with friends.
- You talk and learn when you give presentations.
- You talk and learn when you test yourself by reciting aloud.

Learn by Thinking

- You think and learn in lectures;
  - when you carefully select and record the main points,
  - when relating what is being said to what you already know,
  - when anticipating what the lecturer will talk about

and trying to appreciate his/her approach.

- You think and learn in practical and fieldwork sessions when trying to relate what you are seeing and discovering to what you've learned in your lectures.
- You think and learn when you plan and complete your defined homework.
- You think and learn when you revisit the day's lectures.
- You think and learn when you actively read selected passages from textbooks.
- You think and learn when preparing your study cards.
- You think and learn when you consider your lectures in terms of the course as a whole.
- You think and learn when you prepare for your classes.
- You think and learn when you consider how to attempt past paper questions.
- You think and learn in your final revision when you prepare summary sheets of each of your courses.
- You think and learn in your final revision when you try to predict examination questions and prepare variations of these questions to test yourself.

Summary

I hope that I've shown you in this lesson that by following the advice in this course your learning is greatly enriched compared to a student who takes a passive, negative approach to their studies.

Your learning success is largely determined by your attitude and your study habits. By having a positive, healthy attitude towards your work and by developing good study habits throughout the term, you will *learn, understand,* and *remember* your work with the minimum amount of effort.

Part Four

Feedback Request

Feedback Request

I'd love to hear what you think about this book. Have you found it useful? Did you like one lesson in particular? Maybe you have some ideas as to how the book could be improved?

You can send me your comments at the following email address:

feedback@jadsg.co.uk

I cannot promise to reply to every email, but I do promise to read every one.

It just remains for me to say that I am very grateful to have had the opportunity to share this book with you and I sincerely hope that you have benefited from it.

Finally, I would like to wish you the very best with your studies and for the future.

Best Wishes,

Jason

Dr. Jason A. Davies

Made in the USA
Charleston, SC
13 May 2011